AF489063

Sly's Not a Bad Egg

Written by: R. Elaine Chaklos

Illustrations by: Virginia Humphrey

Candy is definitely not ordinary. She is not ordinary with anything. She thinks everyone has a good side. Candy has a friend who is a jailbird... well, sort of. His name is Sylvester Fox, but his nickname is Sly.

This is his story.

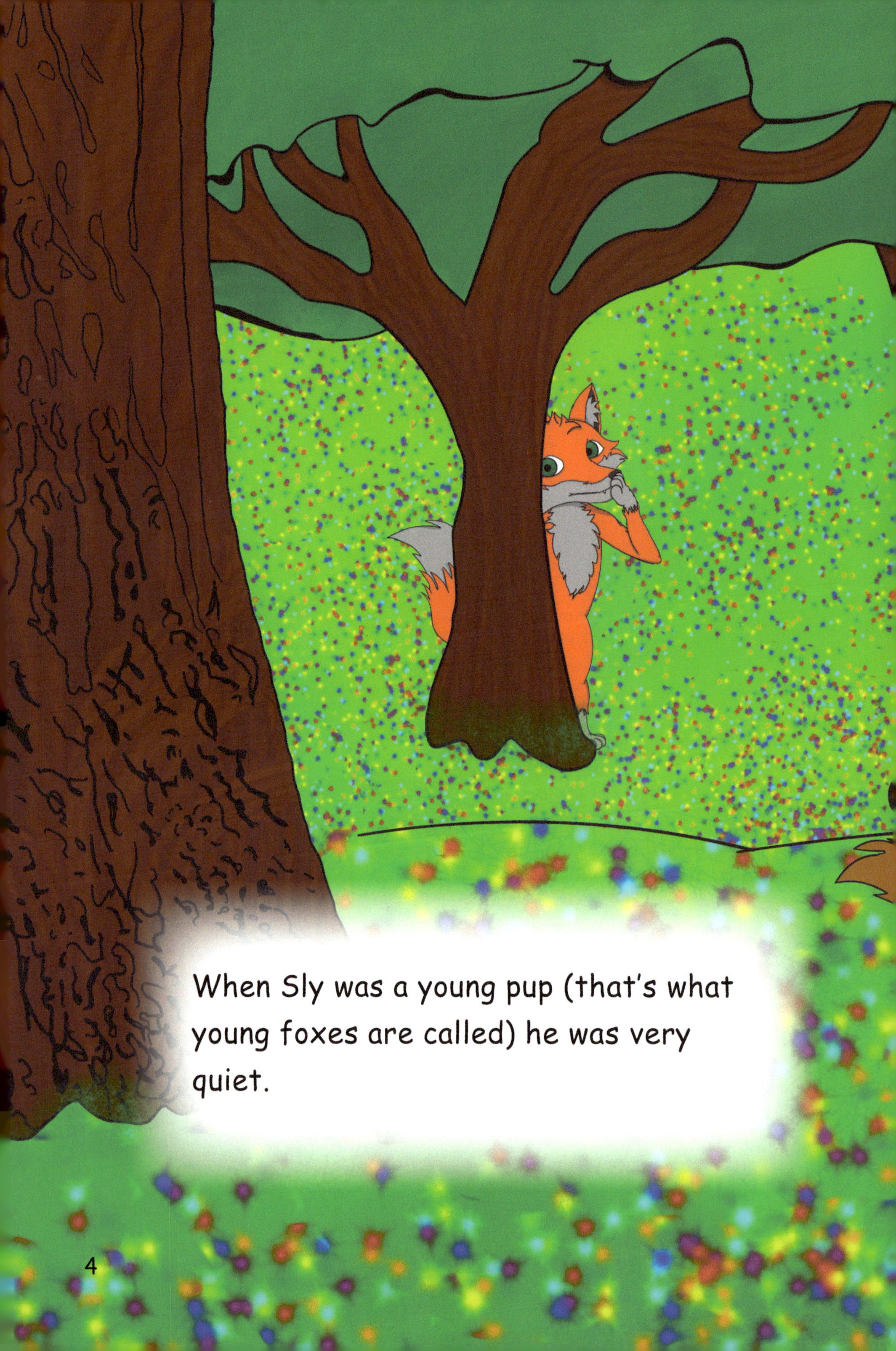

When Sly was a young pup (that's what young foxes are called) he was very quiet.

Because he didn't rough house and play the way other pups did, other animals used to look at him and think he was a bit odd.

After awhile, they said he didn't play with them because he was mean. (Even though he was just shy.)

They started to say he was a bad egg. They didn't know he could hear them, but he could. Foxes have very good hearing, don't you know.

Sly didn't know how to convince the other animals that he was a good egg, so, he decided to start BEING a bad egg.

Sly would disrupt class.

He'd tell his mom he brushed his teeth... when he hadn't.

Sly would interrupt EVERYONE.

Sly would make scary faces at smaller animals.

And he'd tell OBVIOUS fibs.

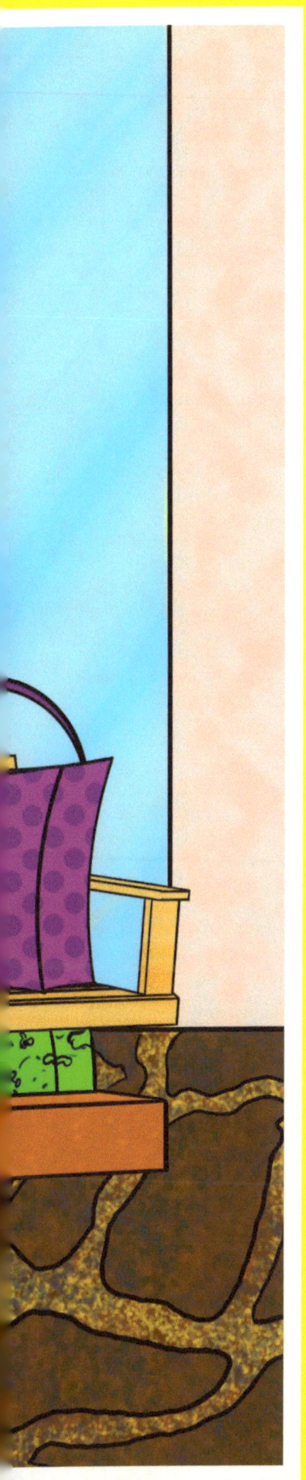

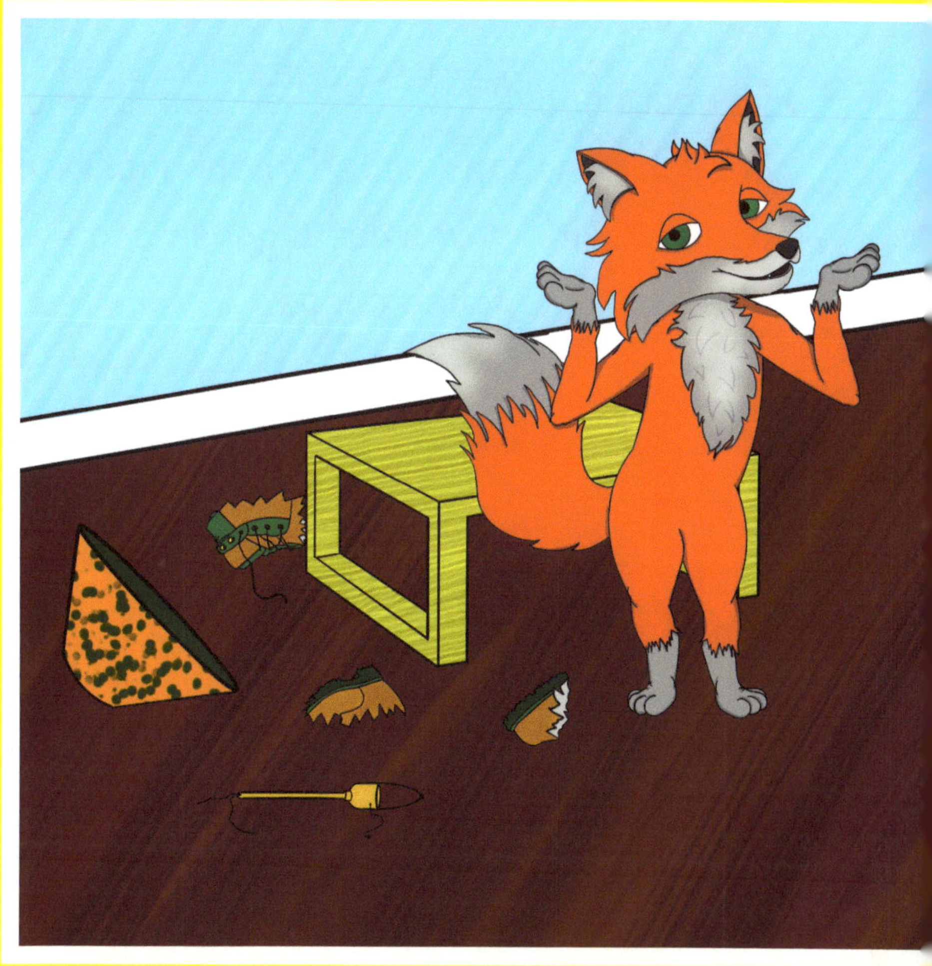

Then he decided he was going to be a REALLY bad egg, and start stealing them. (Eggs that is.)

He would sneak into chicken coops, really goose coops, but nobody called them goose coops because no one would know what a goose coop was, so they called them chicken coops.

Let's just call them plain ol' coops since they are places where both hens and geese lay eggs and sleep.

Well, anyway, after casing the coop, Sly would sneak into the coop when the hens and geese were out picking up bugs for breakfast and before the farmer came out to gather the eggs.

Sly was, well, sly. (Sly and sleepy when he
had to get up, get in, and get out before the
farmers got up!)

And he was selective. He only stole golden eggs, and then only one from a coop.

He always left most of the eggs so nobody would get suspicious. Mr. or Mrs. Farmer then could think the goose would simply have had an off day and didn't lay one.

One time Sly picked the wrong coop to clean out! The wrong hen house to hit! The wrong fowl to foul! Farmer Fred got up early because he had a lot of chores to do that day.

He went into the coop to repair the roost and caught Sly with his hand in the nest.

Oh no! Were they ever surprised! Farmer Fred's tools flew into the air.

Sly's eyes got as big as saucers and when he tried to get away he tripped over a bucket of egg-laying helper. Before he could get his furry feet back under him to flee,

Farmer Fred grabbed him by the tail and texted Sheriff Sharif to come grab the nabber.

Then Sheriff Sharif slammed Sly into
the slammer.

Sly was very remorseful and promised never to take anything that wasn't his ever again. He was released from jail and went straight from then on.

(Sly was released for good behavior. That plus he had a good lawyer!)

Sly was a bad egg, a thief. Well, he used to be one anyway. When Sly got out of jail he decided to turn over a new leaf.

27

He had to work hard to be better.
Changing bad habits is difficult, but he
wanted to be a good egg.

Sometimes he still interrupts other
animals when they are talking, but he
apologizes when he does.

He doesn't disrupt class anymore, partially because
he has already graduated, but mostly because he is
trying to be more polite.

Sometimes he does disrupt moooovies by talking. He
stops as soon as someone reminds him though.

Now he ALWAYS brushes his teeth.

And Sly NEVER takes things that
don't belong to him

Sly isn't perfect, but every day
he tries to be better.

Eventually, a farmer saw what a good egg he'd become and how hard he was trying. The farmer offered Sly a job driving a tractor.

That's how Sly met Candy, but that is a story for another day.

Weeds & Flowers
A Candy Cow Story
Written by: R. Elaine Chaklos
Illustrations by: Virginia Humphrey

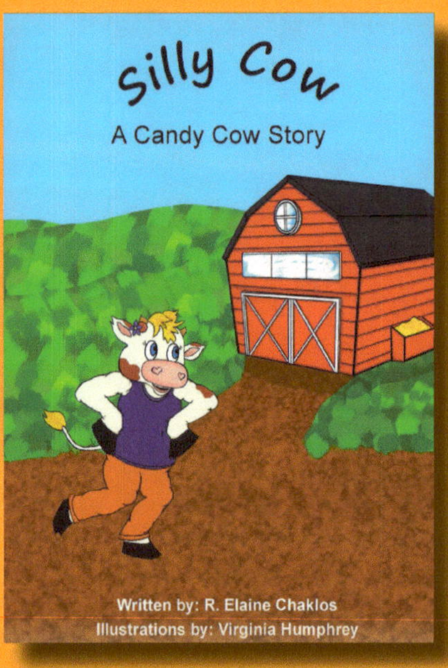
Silly Cow
A Candy Cow Story
Written by: R. Elaine Chaklos
Illustrations by: Virginia Humphrey

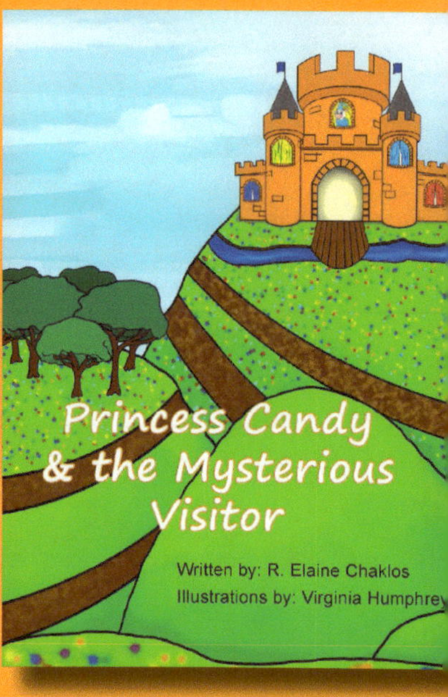
Princess Candy
& the Mysterious
Visitor
Written by: R. Elaine Chaklos
Illustrations by: Virginia Humphrey

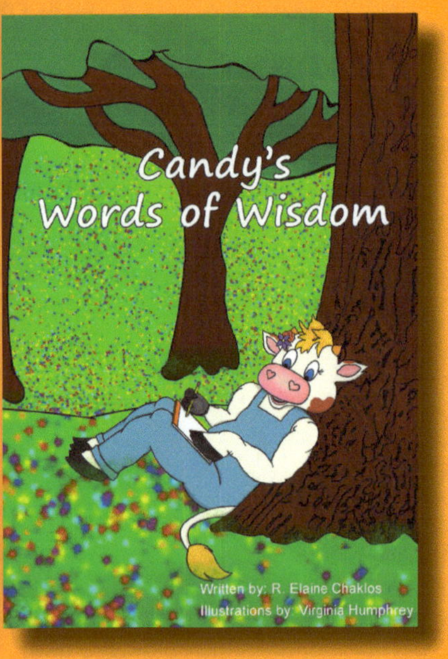
Candy's
Words of Wisdom
Written by: R. Elaine Chaklos
Illustrations by: Virginia Humphrey

Sly's Not
a Bad Egg
A Candy Cow
Story
Written by: R. Elaine Chaklos
Illustrations by: Virginia Humphrey

Candy's
New Friend
Written by: R. Elaine Chaklos
Illustrations by: Virginia Humphrey

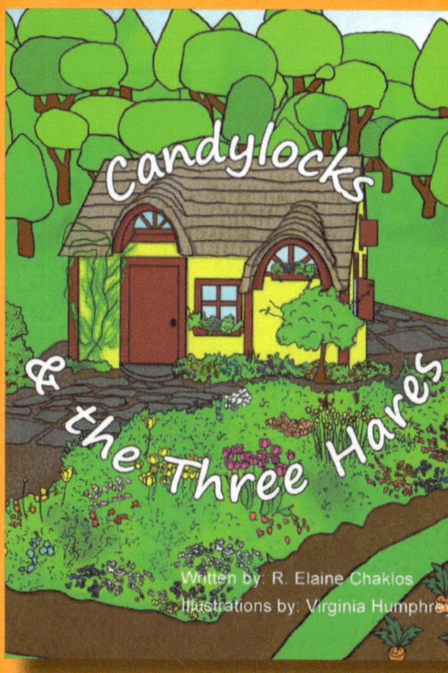

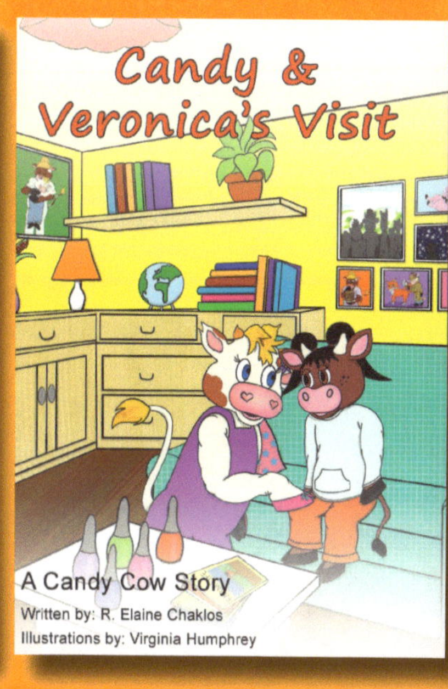

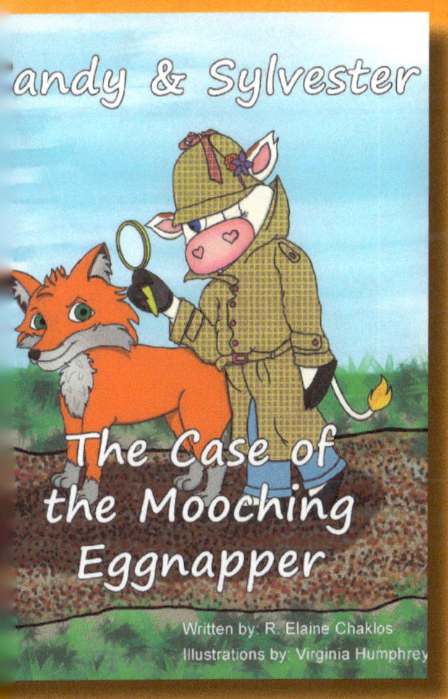

Most of Candy's books have an underlying moral: be the best you, you can be, be what you want to be, no one can make a fool of you without help from you, share, play nice together, etc., but some are just fun.

They are written to make kids and parents smile.

See all of Candy's stories at www.Amazon.com.

MAKE A SLY STATUE
You'll Need: Scissors & a Glue Stick

1. Cut out all the pieces.
2. Slice the tail slot.
3. Glue the body.

4. Fold the feet along the dotted line. Glue the foot tabs onto the inside of the body (so the feet stick out of the body)
5. Put the tail in the Tail Slot.
6. Congratulate yourself. You did it!

Learn more about Candy and her friends and download free activity pages at www.candycow.net.